The Mad Poet's Tea Party

Sandy Jeffs is a Melbourne poet who has published five volumes of poetry and a memoir. Her first book *Poems from the Madhouse* was awarded second place in the FAW Anne Elder poetry prize 1994. Her memoir *Flying with Paper Wings: Reflections on Living with Madness* was shortlisted for the 2010 Age Book of the Year, named SANE Book of the Year 2010 and was commended in the 2010 Human Rights Awards. She has lived with schizophrenia and all its moods since 1976. Sandy has been a public loony for many years presenting as a human face for this often misunderstood condition. She lives with her friends and animals in a place where it's Christmas every day.

ALSO BY SANDY JEFFS

Poems from the Madhouse (Spinifex Press, 1993, 2000, 2002)

Loose Kangaroos (co-author) (The Domain Press, 1998, 1999)

Blood Relations (Spinifex Press, 2000)

Confessions of a Midweek Lady: Tall Tennis Tales (Overthefence Press, 2001, 2009)

The Wings of Angels: A Memoir of Madness (Spinifex Press, 2004)

Flying with Paper Wings: Reflections on Living with Madness (Vulgar Press, 2009, 2010)

Chiaroscuro (Black Pepper Publishing, 2015)

THE MAD POET'S TEA PARTY

Sandy Jeffs

First published by Spinifex Press 2015

Spinifex Press Pty Ltd
504 Queensberry Street
North Melbourne, Victoria 3051
Australia
women@spinifexpress.com.au
www.spinifexpress.com.au

Cover design by Deb Snibson, MAPG
Cover image: Feet Beneath the Table, 1956 © Charles Raymond Blackman.
    Licensed by Viscopy, 2015.
Typeset by Claire Warren
Printed by McPherson's Printing Group

National Library of Australia Cataloguing-in-Publication entry
Jeffs, Sandy, 1953–
The Mad Poet's Tea Party / Sandy Jeffs
9781742199498 (paperback)
9781742199474 (ebook : epub)
9781742199504 (ebook : pdf)
9781742199450 (ebook : Kindle)
    Carroll, Lewis, 1832–1898. Alice's Adventures in Wonderland.
    Mental illness—Poetry.
    Australian poetry—Women authors.
A821.3

PEFC
PEFC/21-31-16

For Sarah and Leigh who made the impossible possible
and Veronica who makes me laugh.

ACKNOWLEDGEMENTS

When *Poems from the Madhouse* was first published in 1993 by Spinifex Press it changed the trajectory of my life in ways I could never have imagined. All the poems in the collection were about the experience of 'madness' as I went from being a 'crazy' person with no purpose, no meaning, no hope and no identity to become recognised as a 'poet'. My purpose had been restored and poetry became an undeniable force in my life. Over the years I have continued to write, in poetry and prose, about madness, seeking to understand its enigmas and contradictions. The poems in *The Mad Poet's Tea Party* are part of this ongoing exploration.

This book could not have come about without the support of the many friends who have allowed me to follow my poetic dreams. Thank you to Lynne and Flick for your enduring friendship. To Leigh and Sarah for your staunch support of my writing and to Veronica, who encouraged me when these poems were tumbling out — this book is dedicated to each of you. I thank Donna Williams for her astute editorial suggestions. My deepest gratitude goes to Robbie and Dido for creating the beautiful sanctuary in which we live and in which I can sit and contemplate poetry. Thank you to Susan and Pauline for your careful and respectful editing of this book. And I thank Susan and Renate and all at Spinifex Press for again taking on the 'mad poet'.

'Medicated' received an Honourable Mention in the 2014 12th Annual BrainStorm Poetry Contest. Some of these poems have appeared in the following: *Poetrix, New Paradigm, Australian Poetry Journal, Open Minds Quarterly, Exploring the Depths* edited by Janette Fernando, the Medical Humanities Blog Site, *Psychopharmacology: Practice and Contexts*, edited by Karen-leigh Edward and Chris Alderman and *Mental Health Nursing: Dimensions of Praxis*, edited by Karen-leigh Edward et al. The quotes from Gudrun Hinze are taken from her poem *Exegesis* first published in the Melbourne Poetry Gig Guide.

CONTENTS

Cogito ergo schizo.

Bruce Plant

The schizophrenic's hell is mental cancer.

David Stewart

What's madness but nobility of soul
At odds with circumstance?

Theodore Roethke

Insanity is a mere disturbance,
like any pressure, it pulls apart...

Gudrun Hinze

Schizophrenics are the proletariat!

Anon
(Seen on a protest banner in the 1960s)

The Madwoman in this Poem

(After Bronwen Wallace)

For Gudrun

> *Yet how stupendous a psychosis*
> *in which God is heard...*
> Gudrun Hinze

The madwoman in this poem
lives on the twenty-second floor
of a block of flats
her husband and children gone
each day she waits for a letter
that never comes
her wrists carry a flurry of scars
her arms are dotted with cigarette burns
every day she contemplates jumping.

The madwoman in this poem
walks the streets
reciting Shakespeare and Milton
she shelters in bus stops and doorways
scrounges through rubbish bins
drinks from discarded beer bottles
begs for money to buy cigarettes
and a moment's respite.

The madwoman in this poem
slumps into a ramshackle chair
hiding herself
her large torpid body founders
her heavy breasts gush

drug-induced lactation
her body grows
with each anti-crazy pill
she reluctantly swallows.

The madwoman in this poem
transfixes in front of the TV
absorbing its many messages
Ally McBeal is her daughter
Eddie McGuire can read her mind
Ridge and Brooke are talking to her
are going to come in a helicopter
take her to Venice to meet Brad Pitt.

The madwoman in this poem
lives in a holy grotto
awaiting the Pilgrims
she carries the burden of Eve
smells God in the toilet
sees the Virgin above the lintel
has given birth to the New Messiah
carries the secret of the Holy Grail in her heart
was raped by the Devil
sees maggots wriggling in her stigmata.

The madwoman in this poem
is sure Beethoven stole the
nine symphonies from her
cannot walk on the cracks of the pavement
can feel spiders eating her brain
fears her head is about to explode
is going to the firing squad next morning

is a character in a Bruegel painting
is an oracle of the dead.

The madwoman in this poem
is everywoman
is any woman
is a mother, daughter
sister, lover, friend —
the madwoman in this poem —
is me.

Sensing Madness

Fateful days beckon
    she loses herself to
        the loosening of her senses
taste is tinged with poison
    hideous sounds sear her ears
        eyes are filled with the Madonna
and the mirror is home to a hag.

This is a time of dark and inglorious days
    as the world looks away while
        her senses sense insane nonsense.

Congratulations

Dedicated to every loopy, loony, schizy out there in la-la land

> *This breakdown of the parts,*
> *neurotransmitters and synapses,*
> *recognises my physicality,*
> *though I am a mental being.*
> Gudrun Hinze

Congratulations!
Now that you are not quite right upstairs
and a candidate for Bedlam
your brain will be malformed
awash with chemical imbalances
the basal ganglia, frontal lobe
limbic system, auditory system
occipital lobe, hippocampus and
neurotransmitters are faulty
there will be structural abnormalities
neurological abnormalities
neuropsychological abnormalities
electrophysiological abnormalities
cerebral metabolic abnormalities
and your brain is almost certain to be
smaller than a healthy one.
Face it you've got a dud brain.

Congratulations!
You have inherited a schizophrenic gene
infectious agents are working away in your body
it could be that your cat caused your lunacy
perhaps a naughty virus has invaded you

your cholinergic system could be in trouble
or you are in need of mega doses of vitamin B3.

Congratulations!
You are having an outburst of homosexual libido
there are repressed sexual complexes
you have an abnormal psychosexual constitution
and we can't dismiss your psychic regression
your loss of ego boundaries
the gross impairment of your reality testing
or your regression to an earlier infantile
phase of psychosexual development.

Congratulations!
You have a disorder of self-experience
involving hyperreflexivity and diminished self-affection
and hypersensitivity to human contact
you are the victim of the
foreclosure of the Name-of-the-Father and
therefore inhabited and possessed by language
don't discount modernity either because
your madness is the product of industrial capitalism
one can't rule out your family driving you mad
especially your mother (don't take it personally)
and the traumas you experienced in childhood
it could be the marijuana you smoked
you may simply be having a sane response to an insane world.

Look, you really are in a bad way
I suggest you have a cup of tea, a Bex and a good lie down
while this psychotic episode passes.

Medicated

Roll up, roll up
join me on the medication trolley
I've been on it for years
I was Largactiled with bitter syrup
I was Pimozided and Melleriled and numbed
I was so Stelazined I was like a cat on a hot tin roof
I've been Modecated into a shuffle
and Clozapined into a stupor
I was Seranaced to drowsiness
and Abilifyed to sleeplessness
when I was Risperidoned I lactated like a cow
they Cogentined me to stop the look ups but I kept looking up
I was Lithiumed and Epilimed to even my pendulum
I've been Imipramined, Prothiadened, Lexaproed
Effexored and Zolofted to happiness
I was Valiumed and Ativaned into tranquillity
at bedtime I was Mogadoned, Stilnoxed and
Temazapamed to slumber-land
now I'm Zyprexaed and ravenous and fuzzled
I'm Lamotrigined and balanced
and Seroquelled
yes indeedy, I'm medicated and dedicated to
the medication trolley
here's looking at you pill bottles.

Cold Chemical Comfort

(After Wislawa Szymborska)

I'm an antipsychotic
I mend broken minds
let me turn your paranoia into trust
your confusion into clarity
I'll expel those voices and
tame your wild delusions
I'll numb your pain and deaden your anxiety
I know how to lighten your load
in the absence of family and friends.

But I have a dark side
I'll make your head feel like it's
stuffed with cotton wool
your ideas will evaporate in a fog
I'll make you crave McDonalds and sugar
have you eating food
like a deranged hog
I'll watch you grow into obesity
with each morsel of me
I'll do away with your desires and urges
your mouth will feel like a sandpit
your hands will tremble
and you'll wobble
you won't shit for days at a time
my kindness will eventually kill you.

But I am your chemical lifeline
give me your madness and

I'll soften it with sedation
just swallow me with water
let my cold chemicals comfort you.

Marinade

My brain is marinating
in a blend of antipsychotics
sanity tastes bitter.

Unquiet Mind

It must be that the mind is elsewhere,
somewhere or nowhere.
Gudrun Hinze

Furled wings
            un-furl-ing
                    (flap & flail)
            furious
    drafts
            whip
                    the uneven air
calm--turns--to--unease
    she is
            t-r-e-m-u-l-o-u-s
    & un-steady
                    drowning in
    (fume & chaos)
            rousing to the
                    command
    of an
            unwelcome presence
overcome by the
                    !!assault!!
            of braying persecution
    reason is
            b-l-e-e-d-i-n-g
            stillness hemorrhages
                    a crack is
            o-p-e-n-i-n-g
    & no light gets in.

Of Shifting Images and Auras

She is a polyphonic song of moving moods
  of shifting images and auras of dreams
her panorama of imagined selves is a
  mythical poly-perception in a transforming world
she is the force for creation and
  the impulse to self-annihilation
she is untouching and untouchable
  the subject and object of her own madness
a towering Babel of psychotic dissonance
  the one who drove Dionysus to madness
who herself is driven mad by him
  she is his delusion and fantasy and
her own delusional polymorphous thought
  she is a flawed work of art in an illuminated
wonderland of rhythms and Humours
  she is a self who is never alone
but she walks alone in the world.

Acrostic #1

For Heidi

The S Factor

Sometimes
craziness creates a
heightened
illumination of the
zeitgeist
originality its
privilege
humour its
revenge
every outsider
nonconformist work of art is an
ingenious
act of lunacy.

Seeing the Insane

*The mad purify us
with their sacrifice*
Elizabeth Campbell

They stand at eternity's gate
gifted by the gods with a *divine madness*—
Crazy Jane, Crazy Ann, Mad Kate
a rake in a madhouse
lunatics dancing at a ball
Charcot's madwomen of Salpêtrière
fools on a ship
Tom O'Bedlam
a knight errant attacking windmills
Tasso imagining *Gerusalemme Conquistata*
Lear *fantastically dressed in wild flowers*
drowned Ophelia
Mad Naomi of *Kaddish*
Dürer's *Melancholia*
the madwoman in the attic
the March Hare and Mad Hatter
Mad Meg at the Gates of Hell
a bewildered face in Goya's *Madhouse*
an inmate in the men's ward at Arles.

They are the fascination of Art
a curiosity of history
a gift to the world
a mirror to our sanity.

Waging War

A mind is a theatre of war
tanks rumble across the synapses
the light horse brigade charges through the frontal lobes
mustard gas poisons serotonin and dopamine
artillery barrages neurotransmitters.
The armies of reason and insanity face off
dispatches from the psych wards report fierce fighting
the casualties are mounting
no prisoners taken.
What will the war memorials say?
They gave their sanity
we honour them.
This is not the war to end all wars.
A mind wages perpetual war—
against itself.

Alice in Larundel Land*

Alice

      fell

           down

                a

                       rabbit hole

    & landed in

                 topsy-turvy Larundel Land

locked up

          captive to lunacy

                 & a passing parade of

       Mad Hatters & March Hares

               eccentrics &

musos & artists & a poet or two

           & ordinary folk

    with the

        d

         e

          e

        p

         e

          s

         t

               sorrows

& in-con-ceiv-able lunacy

              sharing delusions

      like needles

    voices babbling in the background

ECT before breakfast

       stelazine for lunch

          prothiaden for dinner

            melleril at suppertime

& to bed with a hallucination & a moggi
—a place full of hunger—
     hunger for
          —kindness,
               —friendship,
                    —love
a curious, (secluded) world
                        its dark side
  kept well hidden
          shadow-haunted inmates longing for peace
                with themselves
    no one knowing the wars that raged within
or the deep pain wedged between
  (spirit & flesh)
              destroying lives—
friends & family picking up the pieces.

    Larundel Land's
          red brick walls now rubble
windows s-h-a-t-t-e-r-e-d
          graffiti telling another story
    a playground for vandals & urban explorers
          once peaceful gardens
   dis-mem-ber-ed
 sombre ghosts roam the precinct
    calling us to remember them—
we will remember you
    sitting in smoky rooms
             crying alone
    laughing with deranged angels
          —muddled & paranoid
            —chaotic & manic

                                        —anarchic & confused
        prisoners stalking locked wards

                                             keys jangling
            medication trollies
                        r-u-m-b-ling into melancholic rooms
                    & the humour
                                the-blacker-than-black-humour
                the-cut-through-all-the-crap-&-misery-humour
                    you will not be forgotten—
                    we shall erect a monument
                to commemorate all who
                                        passed
        through Larundel Land
                                    we *will* remember
                    the hell-hole & sanctuary
            the bottomless pit of despair
                                unexpected place of healing
            Alice landed on her head
            in upside down
                            Larundel Land
        the madhouse that once stood on the
                                    —edge of town
                where time dawdled
                    & everyone hid in the shadows.

*   *Alice in Larundel Land* is the name of a pantomime that was written by chaplain Len Blair
        and performed by staff at Larundel Psychiatric Hospital in 1979. Larundel was situated in
        the outer Melbourne suburb of Bundoora. It was closed down in 1999.

The Dark Hours

I love the dark hours of my being
My mind deepens into them.
                                    Rilke

come upon me without warning
opening wide the rifts of my mind
their insufferable nights
of reckoning and judgement
endless whimpering self-pity
of a life half lived in regret.

I spend too much time in these hours
my mind darkens into them
a long creep into a deep weeping wound
where I know myself too well
a place of all lost dreams
a place of ever-forming sorrows
a place of a never-ending ache
I see too much
feel too much
labour with my inconsolable self
yield to my sombre mood.

This is a dark hour
in which my soul does not rest in peace
yet a poem is born.

Dangling

The wall between us is very thin.
Why wouldn't a cry from one of us
Break it down?
                    Rilke

The wall between us God is a fortress
we shall never cry to you again
nor hear your cry to us

but if that wall were dismantled
would we meld with your divinity
stand at the gates to the other side

teetering on the edge of perception?
But that is for another time.
It is the paper thin walls

which crumble, we fear madness
calling from behind, shaking
their sheaths, rattling their partitions

stalking us from within
its uninvited companion is acuity.
We walk in the midst of such sharpness

barely holding ourselves together
knowing there is no completeness
in this flood of sensory wakefulness

because as keenness overwhelms us
and the flimsy walls quiver
we dangle from a thread of sanity

while madness snaps at our heels.

Ceaseless Night

The mind is sick tonight.
Raymond Carver

Ah Night, as your dust settles upon us
you bring rest—even to the wicked
but in my room you set your shades upon me
and wrench me from my slumber.

This bed is a rack
and your torturer slowly turns the screw
until a confession is uttered.

No solace in the darkness
only the noise of silence and
the fitful pounding of the heart
and the throb, throb, throb of one's head
and always their bitter recriminations.

To want for peace
but the soul consumes itself
how hard it is to wrestle with the Angel.

O Night, long, unendurable Night
your claw reaches inward
and one lies in frightful wake—
cunning how the dawdling morning
colludes with you
cruel, ceaseless Night.

The mind is sick tonight
and night after night after night
the mind turns on itself—and bites.

The Witching Hour

Stay with me
stay with me awhile
      cradle me in this witching hour
keep your dark brother away
hold the night noise till day.

Stay with me
stay with me awhile
      watch over me in this unruly hour
keep your dark brother away
hold the night noise till day.

Sister Sanity, Lady Sane
stay with me
stay with me awhile
keep your dark brother away
who I'm compelled to obey.

The Burrow

My burrow takes up too much of my thoughts.
                                        Kafka

1

Cautiously she crept out of her burrow
an urge to peal the bells possessed her
she danced on her whimsy and wishes
all was well with the world.

2

Her soul crushed
the flick of an eye
lash of a tongue
curl of a mouth
curse of a word
a cruel recrimination
her soul crushed.

3

Back in her burrow
hiding
sheltering
alone.

4

Her burrow the realm of nightmares
chatterers ridicule and scorn
no silence
no calm
a troubled place!
Her only refuge.

Mental Rape

Can You Hear Them?

I am besieged now
can you hear my enemies
castigating me?

Rasping
my ears with noise
ripping me apart like
Velcro. Cruel, callous mental rape—
heartless.

Calculated pain
death by two angry voices
mean with no conscience.

Crouching Tiger

The crouching tiger
and hidden dragon have come
once more to mock me.
Sniggering as they taunt me
they smear me with their insults.

Vampire

A vampire sucks my
sanity out of me. Crass
devils fill the shell.
Crude beyond belief they shout
abuse. Why can't you hear them?

Occupy My Mind

The loneliest thing I know
Is my own mind at play.
Theodore Roethke

My mind is occupied by
commies, anarchists, socialists
feminists, greenies, liberals
Nazis, fascists, republicans
monarchists, unionists, economic rationalists
tyrants, dictators and despots
there are thieves, conmen
delinquents, murderers, rapists
and other crims in there too
it is occupied by
Jesus, Judas, God, Satan
Tweedledum and Tweedledee
my mind is a full house
I've hung out the 'no vacancy' sign.

My mind is overflowing
full to the brim
chock-a-block
filled up to pussy's bow
with the weightiness of being.

My mind is a dangerous place
an Occ Health and Safety nightmare
put on protective clothing and stand clear because
my mind is occupied by a suicide bomber
and is about to explode.

Caring for My Mind

For Miriam and Lisa

Psychological Dialysis

I talk to my shrink
it's my psychological
dialysis, a

selective diffus-
ion, the separation of
the mad from the sane

keeping the monsters
at bay, holding them back by
caring for my mind.

Soap Opera

I take my soapie
to my shrink. All the gory
details. I need help.

Trust

I give you my mind
and I trust you with my soul—
will it end in tears?

Therapy: Prices Update

Hello!	$~~$10~~	$30
Sit down.	$~~$20~~	$70
How are you?	$~~$30~~	$110
What seems to be the problem?	$~~$40~~	$140
Tell me about it?	$~~$50~~	$190
Could you explain further?	$~~$60~~	$230
Explore your emotions	$~~$70~~	$250
Let's go a bit deeper	$~~$80~~	$290
Be kind to yourself	$~~$90~~	$320
Get in touch with your inner child	$~~$100~~	$360
I hear what you are saying	$~~$110~~	$420
Thank you for sharing that	$~~$120~~	$470
Our time is up	$~~$130~~	$500
Here's a prescription	$~~$140~~	$560
See you next week	$~~$150~~	$630

Next Please!

Hello!	$~~$10~~	$30

Passover

Your cold, callous shadow
passed over us
riding the night's currents
eagle-winged on the mistral
you sucked her soul
her life
her sanity
from her shell
she recoiled
no blood-daubed lintel to spare her
no covenant to protect her.

Deathly Shade
Angel of Insanity
you bleed our senses
you are our curse
our fall
our defeat
you are menace and threat
as you pass over our unguarded door
and seize our minds.

To Melancholia

You moved among us
an unwanted visitor from a dark kingdom
where neither peace nor calm exist
smothering us in your pall
wrapping us in your dreary fancy.

All year long
that long drawn out year
you trailed behind me in a dowdy gown
your breath upon my face—
zephyr from the bowels of the Dark Door.

I repelled you from my gate
you wayward spectre
you soulless ghost from
the city of broken dreams
I repelled you a second time
before my eyes, straining in the dimness
saw you hurtle towards me.

You dragged me into your
Stygian darkness of despair and doubt
where waking day turned into an aching world
of inglorious ways and raggedy days
and all my yesterdays
trailed into a mist of bitter time
and the world stood barren and bare.

Here in this grim and pitiless world
I join my cheerless companions
we are your wretched, Melancholia
Mother of the Black Dog
Dark Queen of the night.

Into the Dark Wood

When day succumbs
to the nightly shroud
her head upon
a beckoning pillow
how utterly spent she feels
how completely drained
    with a cruel weariness of the self.

In heady noise
her plunging mood soaring inwards
to the dark wood—
a horrid place, friendless and sombre
    a place of saddened shades.

Surrendering to the unbeckoned giver
of poisonous potions
she is wrapped in the
    turbid black bile of brooding melancholy.

The Mad Poet's Tea Party

For Donna

The Loony in the Pack

The belfry bats are doing my head in
one eye sees Yin
the other eye Yang.

I go to bed an angel
and wake up a demon
I thought I was a sunrise
then discovered I was a sunset
yesterday I was a princess
today a pauper.

But I'm no Jekyll and Hyde
just the iceberg of the tip
there's more behind my iron curtain
than meets the eye
maybe I'm the loony in the pack.

Party Time

The loose roos are raising my roof
it's their party time
they're hanging me out to dry
but I'm hanging tough even though
I'm on a slippery slope to nowhere
because I keep missing the bus

I'm on a highway to the funny farm
and a stairway to the bughouse
but it's no use crying over spilt sanity.

Smoke & Mirrors

I'm on the shelf with a cut snake
up a pole and out of my tree
the world has been taken out of my oyster
I'm on the inside looking out
through my mind's eye
but I can't get my head around it
I can't make head nor tail of it
so I'm casting my mind back to a time
before the slings and arrows of craziness
to find the hypodermic needle in the haystack
but life wasn't meant to be sane
so I'm pulling my socks up
and trying to get a life
in spite of the smoke and mirrors of lunacy.

Loose Screw

Is it simply a question of matter over mind
of things crossing my mind
having a mind open to anything
of being out of my cotton-pickin' mind
is my mind's eye too vivid or too clouded
are there too many butterflies in it
do I only have half a mind to do anything
or am I heels over head with a screw loose?

The Eye of the Beholder

Cheer up because every mad cloud has a sane lining
and every sane cloud has a mad lining
and I'm from the school of hard rocks where
sanity is in the eye of the beholder and
lunacy is in the eye of a shrink.

Tea Party

I must be as silly as a wheel
because I'm in seventh heaven
sipping tea at the mad poet's tea party
far from the madding crowd
in cloud-cuckoo land
on a slow boat to Bedlam
where the reality of madness is surpassed by
the madness of reality.

Acrostic #2

The Self You Fear

Since sanity is in the eye of the beholder
cast your mind back to
how you treated the madwoman
in the crowd doing
zany things
others mocked her
perhaps you laughed, perhaps you cried
have you thought about it?
remember, when you next see me
entertaining the crowd
notice my face, look into my eyes
I am your doppelganger, your
curious self you fear the most.

Perhaps I scare you
since I take
you to places you never knew
care for me
hold me in your heart
open your eyes
to the world beyond
I am your guide
come fly with me on lunacy's wings.

Seroquelled

The rumours circulating from the madhouse
reported that the inmates were
taking over the asylum
the medication wasn't working
and the nurses and doctors had barricaded
themselves in the fishbowl
when the uprising was seroquelled
the mad comrades were exiled
they are sending postcards from their seclusion rooms.

SuperMadwoman

Madder than a mad dog
more deluded than God
able to hallucinate the Virgin Mary with a golden aura
look, up in the sky
it's a bird, it's a plane
it's Super*Mad*woman!
yes, it's Super*Mad*woman—
strange visitor from another reality
who came to earth with thoughts and theories
far beyond those with ordinary minds
Super*Mad*woman—
who can change the course of mighty universes
bend ideas with her unhinged mind
and who, disguised as Sandy Jeffs
mild-mannered sane woman
from a quaint outer suburban household
fights the never ending battle
for lunacy, unreason
and the subversive way!

I Peeped

Suddenly she froze
her song hushed
her eyes closed
she drew me into her vision.

I saw a glowering twisted face
an angular chin and
pock-marked skin
she stared at me with
searing blood-red eyes
her incandescent tangled hair
juddered wildly
and laughter, raucous, riotous laughter
laced with obscenities and ridicule.

I had peeped into her imagination
and saw horror, pure horror
and a darkened mind—
hers or mine?

How?

How did this Madwoman
step into my shoes
and walk me along the
road of jagged thoughts?

How did this Madwoman
cut my jugular
then watch my mind bleed?

How did this Madwoman
pick the lock and
thieve my sanity?

I thought I would sail away
into the sunset and
be assured of a safe trip
instead I was set upon
by this Madwoman
who stole my mind
and sold it like a
piece of cheap real estate—
how?

Solitude

Will someone enter my solitude
Dorothy Hewett

She always wanted
    —someone—
        to enter her
    [[solitude]]
    open--her--mind's--gate
        let out the demons
E-X-C-O-R-I-A-T-E the voices &
ven-til-ate the
        [[polluted thoughts]].

She always wanted
    —someone—
        to fill the d-e-e-p hole of
l-o-n-g-i-n-g
        salvage the wreckage &
R-E-S-U-S-C-I-T-A-T-E
her
        [[soul]].

Awakening

For Nev

But sleeping is no state for lunatics
Mal McKimmie

When we mad awaken
and sever the noose of shame
when we lift our heads high and
draw ourselves torn at heart
from the well of madness
when we show our faces to the world
haggard and worldly-wise
will the world be welcoming?

When we mad awaken
and reflect on all that has happened
remembering the times before
the loosening of our minds
will our mind-chains be unleashed?

When we mad awaken
shaken and battered from our nightmares
our lives dangling between worlds
will our cracked minds open to light?

When we mad awaken
we will fling open the seclusion doors
out we will surge like waters unstopped
and all our tortured yesterdays will disappear
when we mad awaken, beware!

Spirals

1

They say I am damaged DNA
the helix curled and twirled
its double strands twisted
chains broken
code bungled
the wrong information given
something awful attached itself to my biology
chemical imbalances are everywhere
I am a somatic disaster
a site of cerebral annihilation.

2

Intruders assault me
voices up, me down
voices down, me up
mood up, me up
mood down, me down
mood grandiose, me inflated
mood paranoid, me deflated
spiral up, coil down
me up, me down
spiral down, coil up
me down, me up.

3

They want to unravel my ravel
unwind my mind
untangle my spirals
re-programme the code
undo my DNA.
Do I need a double felix
to heal my damaged double helix?

McMadness

Hello, do you have a Big Mac delusion
or a Cheeseburger delusion?
Is that one voice with grandiose ideas
or two voices of persecution?
Have you spent all your savings
and bought three new Ferraris and a Rolls lately
and slept with every Tom, Dick and Jane?
Are you self harming or
feeling unremitting misery?
Then drive thru the *fast*psychiatry ward
we'll have you McDiagnosed,
treated, medicated and McSane
in two shakes of a pill bottle
and by the way, if your suicidal threats
are only attention seeking
leave now because you are wasting our time
McSanity is our business.

Now that you are here
terms and conditions apply
you can only stay a few days
but don't worry we'll get you McSane
before you can say
can I have some compassion with that?
We'll give you drugs that will fatten you up
kill your libido
make you dribble and constipated
turn you into a zombie
sedate to you to exhaustion
eventually bring on diabetes

cardiovascular disease
and premature death.
We'll have you out of here like shit off a shovel
even if you're still mad
because there'll be someone madder who will need your bed
but don't worry we'll give you a McHappy Pack
full of pharmaceutical goodies
free of charge to take with you
and just to make sure you are somewhere in the system
and can't do a runner and not get treatment
we'll slap a Community Treatment Order on you
and we'll offer you McTherapy
to help you cope with isolation
unemployment, poverty and rejection
we'll have you McSane if it kills you.

And now for some McTherapy:
hello
how are the voices today?
keep taking the medication
we have to finish now
do you need a prescription?
credit or savings?
see you in 6 months.

So, he's McSane and out of the bin
and back in your care
how wonderful that you can experience
deep emotional fulfilment
by looking after your psychotic son 24/7
with no support and no resources
while you hold down a job and

try to keep your family happy
your marriage intact and
not lose your friends.
Don't worry if you can't cope when he is
threatening to kill himself
the CAT team might pop in a couple of times a day
just to make sure things are okey-dokey
you'll survive the other 23 hours
of worry and stress and doing the best you can
in an impossible situation because
you always do and because you love him
and if you are desperate *you* can have some McTherapy too
because your McSanity is important.

It's a McMad world
everyone has forms to fill in and boxes to tick
i's to dot and t's to cross
performance requirements to meet
risk assessments to make
& pressure, pressure, pressure
*Fast*psychiatry is the name of this game
Ah, McSane we've done it again.

I Called You Mad

(After Geoff Prince)

For 'Greg'

I called you *mad*
when you were spellbound to the
full-throated voices of accusation
and held captive by the ecstasy
of untamed delusions.

I called you *mad*
when you lost yourself
in dark melancholy
ordained to move as a silhouette
over the world.

I called you *mad*
and damned you to your demons and
sucked your soul dry
with quackery and potions
then swept you under the carpet.

I called you *mad*
and cast you off on the Ship of Fools
to roam the world in exile
condemned to be scorned
and ridiculed.

I will remember you
because I called you *mad*
in a moment of folly—
you are only a fool
in the eyes of the foolish.

I called you *mad*
you will regret that.

There's Something Dead in My House

There's something
          //DEAD// in my house
     its rancid stench cuts // the air
                    strips paint // off walls
it s-u-p-p-u-r-a-t-e-s
          under // floor boards
     swills in my toilet
its rotting flesh   h
                      a
                      n
                      g
                      s
                    off //grey// bones
     MAGGOTS wriggle in
c-o-n-g-e-a-l-i-n-g   //juices//.

There's something
          //DEAD// in my house
     I can taste the   <decay>
          see the   f-e-s-t-e-r
     touch the c-o-n-g-e-a-l-i-n-g // blood
          hear the ravenous   MAGGOTS
smell the // putrid // flesh.

There's something
          //DEAD// in my house—
                         //me?//

When They Came To Get You

*Whoever you are – I have always depended on
the kindness of strangers.*
Tennessee Williams

When they came to get you
waving their credentials
and certification papers
offering duplicitous hands—

When they came to get you
I held your hand
brushed your troubled brow
walked with you—

When they came to get you
they came for me too.

I Am Not the Same Person

That person I once was and
the person I am now
are not the same
we do not share the same feelings
the same body, the same mind
my eyes are not my own
I do not see the world as I once did
even friends have a different complexion.

I understood my ancient darkness
it was a misery I knew well
now a stranger walks in my old shoes
and wears the ragbag clothes I once wore.

I want for the wind to blow a wisp
of recognition across my face
to whisper in my ears a familiar sound
and reacquaint me with my former self
for now I have no evidence of who I was.

Whoever is watching over me
sustain me in this midnight hour of estrangement
and rescue me from this person I have become
I neither know nor like.

Surgery of the Soul*

Here rueful-visaged angels seem to tell,
With weeping eyes, a soul is gone to hell.
Thomas Chatterton

This soul is in poor health
this soul is a waste land
this soul is a labyrinth
this soul is a parasite
this soul is mendacious
this soul is Dorian Gray's picture
this soul is Mr Kurtz's horror
this soul is angry and unattractive
this soul is the Tree of Knowledge
this soul can be bought
this soul is drowning in guilt
this soul is soulless
this soul is possessed
this soul is broken
this soul needs a lobotomy.

* Walter Freeman pioneered lobotomy in the USA which *The New York Times* hailed as 'Surgery of the Soul'.

Threadbare

From   the   cradle
    piece--by--piece
             she was
     r-i-p-p-e-d
            to
                   s-h-r-e-d-s
bit--by--bit
        the threads were
     u-n-r-a-v-e-l-l-e-d
             odds & ends
       flew
     c-h-a-o-t-i-c-a-l-l-y
             she tried to
(gather the filaments in a ball)
        but
the strands were
        too many to
    mend her
t-h-r-e-a-d-b-a-r-e
           life.

Calculating the Cost

She sees herself in a shadow she once loved
at a time when her small hands hugged to her chest
her lightness of being.

How long, long ago it was
when in her infant heart she hoped
her ever ripening core would one day bear fruit.

But the carapace of infancy was too brittle
now she is a silhouette eclipsed in her childhood sadness
and the once-loved shadow is unloved.

She is plummeting into an unfathomable hollowness
asking herself as she collides with her corroded core
what is this unnamed guilt?

Why such heaviness of being?
Why the ceaseless despondency?
She is calculating the cost of her own dislike.

Suicide

Fruit clings
as it grows and ripens.

Some fruit clings so tightly
it is hard to harvest.

Some fruit lets go easily
plummeting before it has ripened.

Perhaps the tree was unwell
or the fruit was rotten.

Perhaps birds had pecked its flesh
or insects had eaten its core.

Perhaps it had been weakened by a bad season
or damaged by a storm.

A fruit let go
why?

Staying Alive

Hanging by a Thread

Hanging by a thread
what is keeping me alive?
Inexplicable.

Life is a Game of Tennis

Should have been over
in three sets. It's gone to five.
Miracles happen.

To Be or Not To Be

Top myself, have brekkie...
hanging between the living and the dead

the thread weakens.
Top myself, have brekkie...

She has hung between the living and the dead
too many times

the dead always calling
the living undeserving of her.

What pushes one over the edge—
a recrimination, a slice of anger

being a burden, no way out
the way too lonely

the end too near to pull back from?
Top myself, have brekkie...

She lies in bed mouthing her morning mantra
top myself, have brekkie, top myself, have brekkie...

have brekkie...yes...have brekkie...
But tomorrow?

Beggar

Begging for sanity
requires strength

A mind not wearied
from the struggle

A mind not spent
of its force

Begging for sanity
is an unacknowledged struggle

To not surrender to a mad god.

Housemate

I live with schizophrenia
and all her moods
she is the housemate from hell.

Downsizing

I'm downsizing my mind
in preparation for the new year
I'm chucking out my delusions
giving my voices the boot
telling the hag in the mirror to fuck off
ditching the neurotic anxiety
packing off the insomnia to slumber-land
downgrading the hypomania to serenity
upgrading the depression to joy
off-loading the baggage
turning agitation into stillness
redirecting my anger away from myself
simplifying my thought processes
stopping the intellectualisation of everything
putting up a barrier to the world and
having a rest from pessimism.

But if I downsize my mind
will I be downsizing my poetry?

The Social Worker

The social worker
    thought I was cactus
a dead loss
    a blight on the world.
She said I had reached
    the end of the line.
I believed her
    thought I was history
a story with a crappy ending
    a nobody who
walked in the shadows of others
    and cast none of my own
a witch who made others miserable
    a carbuncle on my friends' lives.
I had reached *the end of the line*
    so the social worker from hell said
condemning me to another hell
    which had nothing to do with being mad.

Where is the Rage?

As she turns the pages of her life
they appear blank of rage.

Where is the rage of the little girl
who watched her father rage?

Where is the rage of the little girl
who drowned in her mother's alcohol?

Where is the rage of the little girl
who was raped?

Where is the rage of the young woman
gone mad?

Where is the outrageous rage?

Here lies rage
in the rupturing claw of self-hatred.

Here lies the rage
in a heart boiling with rage.

Here lies the rage
in a rage too dangerous to let loose.

Here lies the rage
in the voices that rage at her.

Here lies the rage
in the fear of rage.

Here lies the rage
buried in pages of poetry—

It is all she can do to hold back the rage.

The Sanity App

Are you in a difficult relationship?
do you work in a stressful environment?
do you find modern life too overwhelming?
do you have a history of madness?
do you worry about your sanity?
then we have the solution for you.

The Sanity App offers you the chance to
assess your sanity 24/7
don't be dependent on a psychiatrist
be your own shrink
reassure yourself you are sane
this portable sanity test can be used anywhere:
in meetings
at playgroup
dealing with teenagers
in the classroom
at the footy
if you discover your partner is having an affair
endeavouring to understand the logic of your computer
on the tennis court
listening to talkback radio
watching reality TV
if you are having a senior moment
trying to decode bureau-babble and legalese
hearing a politician
if you find yourself wishing you were Kim Kardashian
driving
getting messages from God.

Questions are the standard ones used in a clinical setting
but we have modified some of them
to be iPhone user friendly such as:
easy to decipher proverbs
counting back from 100 in 2s only
hints as to who might be the current Prime Minister.

Special features include:
an easy menu so you can use it while under stress
quick check delusion register
voices recognition validation
hallucination authenticator
a paranoia scale
reality checks.

If you score badly and your sanity is shown to be failing
we have the numbers of CAT teams so they can come and get you
phone numbers and addresses of psychiatrists
locations of public hospital psychiatric wards
so you can present yourself there for treatment
and there are suggestions on what to say to ensure you are admitted.

It comes with preventative action plans
to stave off madness with recommendations for:
natural remedies
yoga positions
relaxation and meditation exercises
and stress management tools.

It also has a diagnostic menu so you can
identify what type of madness you are suffering.

You can rate the Sanity App
some customer ratings:
Gavin: I gave it 5 stars because it got me to a psych ward
before I topped myself
Sharon: It was good but I only gave it 3 stars because I couldn't
get rid of the Virgin Mary.

Requirements: iPhone, iPod touch and iPad.

Category: Lifestyle

Rated 9+ for the following:
suggestive themes

The Sanity App costs a cheap $1.99 because
we know how valuable your sanity is.

Done to Death

(After Andy Kissane)

I'm a little concerned
I've done madness to death
and I'm casting around for another subject
to engage my interest
but I *am* madness
and madness *is* me
it holds you captive
like a hapless bunny
caught in the headlights.

A Life

A life is only a breath
shallow at times
barely feathering the cheeks
of one's companions
who share the way.

When they frame the shadows of
the nether world in a golden cage
into which she comes brittle and
from which she leaves mad
let them say:
she was the maddest of all
and she shall say:
my life was only a breath
a hush and a crescendo
that fell upon a deaf world.

Loonies of the World Unite!

If you would like to know more about Spinifex Press, write for
a free catalogue, email us for a PDF, or visit our website.

Spinifex Press
PO Box 212, North Melbourne
Vic. 3051 Australia
www.spinifexpress.com.au

Many Spinifex books are now also available as eBooks.
See the eBookstore on the Spinifex website for more details.